GW00541122

Dundee in old picture postcards

by Norman Watson

European Library ZALTBOMMEL / THE NETHERLANDS

The Author:

Norman Watson was born and brought up in Perth. He is a journalist with The Courier in Dundee. He was the author of The Courier Book of Dundee (1990) and his other publications include Dundee Suffragettes (1990), Perth in Postcards (1991), Perth in old picture postcards for the European Library series (1993), The History of The Pow of Inchaffray (1997) and Daughters of Dundee (1997). An honours graduate, he is currently completing a part-time PhD in political science with the Open University / Edinburgh University.

Acknowledgements:

Grateful thanks to Angela Mathers and to Linda McGill for their help in the preparation of the text, and to D.C. Thomson and Co, Ltd, Dundee, for assistance with a number of photographs. The majority of postcards are from the author's collection.

GB ISBN 90 288 6404 0

Introduction

Dundee established itself by enterprise and energy. It built its harbours and docks and harnessed to its purposes the waters of the River Tay, just seven miles from the sea. It pioneered trading routes to the Baltic and established the greatest whaling fleet in the Empire. Its heroic manufacturing output made Dundee the second city in Scotland and the world's centre of jute production. The triumph of jute – or King Jute as the Dundee Advertiser declared in 1872 – impacted on the town's population, which rose dramatically from 26,000 in 1800 to 160,000 in 1901. By 1872 over seventy mills employed 40,000 people, almost 30,000 of them women and girls. During the First World War, Dundee's staple industry supplied 150 million sandbags in a single fortnight in a response to a desperate appeal from London.

The jute boom coincided with the Golden Age of the picture postcard. From its Perth Road works the firm of James Valentine and Sons became one of Britain's largest postcard producers. The company was started in Dundee by John Valentine in 1825, but it was the founder's great-grandson Harben Valentine, who joined in 1886, who took advantage of the ending of the Government monopoly on postcards in 1894, and the granting of permission in 1897 to write or print on their reverse side. Millions were produced in Dundee. Although Valentine's ceased postcard production in 1970, another postcard pioneer, J.B. White of Dundee, continues to this day in the form of Whiteholme Ltd.

The doubling of the price of sending a postcard from $^1/_2$d to 1d in 1918, and the extension of the telephone, contributed to the demise of the postcard in inter-war years, but not before it had reflected on Dundee's grim industrial age, with scenes of tenements reminiscent of Dickens' semi-mythical Coketown. Similarly, Dundee's greatest industry went into decline, but not before Broughty Ferry, three miles east of Dundee, where many of the jute barons had built fantastic mansions, was absorbed into the city. In 1806 the Dundee Advertiser stated that Broughty Ferry was attracting large numbers of visitors due to its excellent beach and seaside location. It was described as the 'Brighton of the North' – though no-one having visited both could have possibly thought them similar. But at one point, 100 trams at day passed backwards and forwards to Dundee from its new suburb.

Meanwhile, with inter-war unemployment at 30% in Dundee as a whole and 50% in the jute industry, Dundee's energies bent towards a new industrial era as generations of provenly dextrous inhabitants rose to the challenge of the electronic age, supporting the arrival of firms such as Timex and NCR. But the city's wealth had come from jute, and the magnates' legacy was patronage and benevolence, as witnessed by postcards of gifts such as Baxter Park, Caird Hall and the Albert Institute.

Meanwhile, major new housing developments, such as Logie, Craigiebank and Clepington, to be followed by the sprawling estates on the city's periphery, were transforming the physical character of the city, and Dundee cleared away much that was squalid. It has also survived the trauma of a fallen rail bridge, built another and opened a road crossing to Fife. More recently it has turned to tourism and amassed considerable international standing for its maritime history. Importantly, it is now a two-university city with a medical school of world repute.
And today, ninety years after the Golden Age of the picture post-cards, once-familiar mills, ships, buildings and streets have taken on new appearances and exciting functions. Similarly, attics around the city have given up hidden hoards of Edwardian postcards, chronicling the life and times of Dundee. This is their legacy in pictures.

1 This fine High Street scene shows Dundee's first Sunday tram car on 10th September 1905, on its journey towards Ninewells, obviously brim full for the run westwards along the High Street. In order to prevent disturbances during church services, Dundee's first Sunday tram did not run between 11 a.m. and just after noon.

2 Now we see the Sunday tram in the Nethergate, travelling eastwards to the High Street. When electric trams were introduced in 1905, many people claimed they were blinded by the lighting inside after the dim, funereal glow of the horse-drawn era. Trams were withdrawn from Dundee in 1956.

3 This Valentine's study of Clepington Road at the turn of the century provides a tranquil scene hardly likely to be repeated in today's rush hour. Note the elegant gas lamps and the sophisticated Venetian blinds in the window above Fairmuir Post Office.

4 This photograph shows a Bleriot monoplane in the Stannergate around 1910. Dundee's own pioneering aviator was Preston Watson. Watson was said by witnesses to have made a powered flight above Errol 'in the summer of 1903.' This led to many years of debate over whether the young Dundonian actually preceded the Wright Brothers into the air.
Preston Watson died in 1915 while on service with the Royal Flying Corps.

5 D. M. Brown had a romantic growth from a single-windowed shop at 80 High Street to the magnificent arcade shown here. Why an arcade? There is a story that D. M. Brown, having acquired a Commercial Street frontage in addition to his premises in the High Street, wanted to join the two by 'turning the corner'. He was frustrated, however, by the chemist in the corner site who demanded an exorbitant price for his stance. Brown's answer was to make a continuous row of display windows under cover running behind the corner.

6 The Alexandra drinking fountain was formerly one of the city's most popular meeting places. It was presented by Lord Provost William Longair to commemorate two Royal visits to Dundee in 1907 and 1908 – happily for us, both recorded during the Golden Age of the picture postcard. More recently, the fountain looked a lost soul as the area in front of the old Caledonian station (seen in the background) was transformed into the Discovery Quay approach area.

7 There was a strong rivalry between the Barony of Hilltown and the Burgh of Dundee in ancient times. At one point trade between the two was banned. The purchase of the Barony by the Burgh in 1699 was a major factor in settling old scores. But the Hilltown preserved both its identity and its colourful culture. The Hilltown's most famous landmark today (apart from the supermarket!) is the tap-o'-the-hill clock, seen here in the background. It was presented by Dundee's Lord Provost in 1900, presumably as a peace offering.

8 Dundee Trades Hall was built in 1776 and enlarged in 1851. Its original rusticated ground floor is illustrated in Lamb's Dundee. It was built as the meeting place of the Nine Incorporated Trades of Dundee. When it was demolished in 1878, as a consequence of changes initiated by the 1871 Improvement Act, a unique painted plaster frieze, showing a traditional parade performed by the Cordiner Trade (shoemakers), was rescued and given to Dundee Museum.

9 The Royal Dundee Institution for the Blind was opened in Magdalen Green in 1885. It benefited from electric power in 1912 and from a visit from King George two years later. A year after that the title 'Royal' was awarded. One of the institution's main objectives was to provide employment for adult blind persons. A retail shop in the city's Nethergate was opened in 1964 to display their work. By then the institution employed 130 workers.

10 Dundee's Royal Arch was actually Royal Arch II – the sequel. The first was constructed of wood and erected in 1844 in celebration of Queen Victoria's visit to the city. In 1850 it was decided to establish a more lasting commemoration of the visit in stone. The arch, a landmark to seafarers, not to mention generations of Dundonians, was demolished in 1964 to make way for the Tay Road Bridge.

11 This postcard shows a west-bound tram passing Sinderins corner around 1920. Blackness Library, seen on the right, was the gift of the wealthy philanthropist Andrew Carnegie, who provided £37,000 to build and equip several libraries in the city. It was designed by Dundee's innovative city architect James Thomson and opened in 1908.

12 The Albert Institute was designed by Sir George Gilbert Scott, one of the foremost architects of his era. The Library department opened in 1869 and the Museum and Art Galleries followed in 1873. In 1978 the Albert Institute began a new phase when the public library left the building to move to the Wellgate. The meadow area which once existed in front of the building was the city's open-air forum – the rendezvous of would-be politicians and fire and brimstone gospellers!

13 Dundee Town House was designed by William Adam, father of the famous Adam brothers, in 1734. The building was steeped in history. It witnessed an attempt by the Jacobites to return to power under Bonnie Prince Charlie in 1745. Towards the end of the 18th century it saw public protests inspired by the French Revolution. In 1803, when Napoleon threatened invasion, the Provost mustered the Dundee Volunteers at its doors. Then, in 1832, rioters attempted to set fire to the building to 'burn out the Tories'. The Town House was controversially demolished in 1932.

14 Raphael Tuck's famous Oilette series were among the Rolls-Royces of postcards. This splendid beach scene at Broughty Ferry is a typical example of the Tuck treatment. The artist is David Small, a local man who worked for major publishers.

15 The King's Theatre, later the Gaumont, was built in 1908. Since it closed as a cinema and, latterly, as a bingo hall, much has been said about the building's future. During its heyday as a theatre, however, it boasted twice nightly performances and, as this fine Edwardian postcard shows, it drew the crowds.

16 The one-time importance of Court House Square, now rather peripheralised on the margins of the city centre, can be gauged by this postcard. From the left we see the Salvation Army hostel, the bus terminus, the façade of the Sheriff Court and the main entrance to the Central Hotel. The Palladian-style court house, which included the police office and jail, was built in 1833. The former hotel is now banking offices.

17 The old Albert Square post office stood at the top of Reform Street, opposite the main gates of Dundee High School. It opened in 1862 and formed the focal point of the rapidly developing city postal service for thirty years. This expansion soon led to the need for new and larger premises and the office seen in this postcard was demolished in 1898.

18 The central section of the first Tay Bridge collapsed during a terrible storm on 28th December 1879. No one survived. Locomotive 244 was salvaged from the river the following April. The heavy lifting chains broke twice during the operation. Given the tragic circumstances, it is curious today to learn that the engine was returned to service and remained in use until 1917. The macabre nickname given to it by railwaymen was 'The Diver'.

OLD TAY BRIDGE DISASTER, 1879: THE ENGINE

19 The Central Reading Rooms in Barrack Street date from 1911 and were created out of Andrew Carnegie's global drive to improve library facilities. The building is now Barrack Street Museum and features the city's natural history collections, including the famous Tay Whale skeleton. Barrack Street was formerly Burial Wynd. In April 1807 its residents, perhaps not surprisingly, petitioned the Town Council to have the name changed.

20 The estate of Dudhope was granted by Sir William Wallace to Alexander Scrymgeour when he was appointed Constable of Dundee in 1298. The original keep was replaced by a castle in the 15th century, which in turn was replaced by the existing building a century later. Although Dudhope Castle's walls are many feet thick, Dundee's militant suffragettes took the notion to blow it up in 1914 – only to see the fuses to their explosives extinguished by a breeze!

21 A shambles of slaughter houses existed at the head of the Murraygate, in the far distance in this splendid postcard. A weekly horse market was once held in the vicinity. It is recorded that the animals were raced up and down the congested thoroughfares to the great danger of the inhabitants. It was in the Seagate adjoining the Murraygate that Dundee's infamous witch, Grizzel Jaffray, was burned at the stake in 1668.

22 The magnificent Clydesdale Bank building has dominated the heart of the High Street for 120 years and was the talk of the town when it gave the first public demonstration of electric light. Down the Murraygate, on the left, was another building equally popular on pay-day Fridays – the La Scala cinema. This was opened in 1913 and pioneered 'talkies' when they were introduced to Dundee in 1930.

23 Although this postcard refers to the site of Mathers' temperance hotel, generations of Dundonians knew the building as the Cholera Hospital. It was just a tenement when it was commandeered by the city's health authorities when the infirmary in King Street couldn't cope with cholera victims during a major outbreak in 1832. During the epidemic Magistrates ordered tar barrels to be burned in the streets to purify the air.

24 This view of the High Street and Bridge Lochee, featuring the Old Toll Bar, dates from 1913. It will be a scene readily familiar to all those with connections past or present to the Camperdown jute works nearby. Lochee High Street was also a busy terminus for trams.

HIGH STREET, SHOWING RAILWAY BRIDGE, LOCHEE

25 This pre-1900 harbour scene shows the Royal Arch on the left and the docks extending up to Shore Terrace and George Morton's bonded warehouse, now the subject of a sensitive conversion into flatted accommodation. Morton's began life as a grocery business in 1838. Rubble from the demolition of the Royal Arch in 1964 was used to fill Earl Grey Dock nearby. Many were keen to see the back of it – its nicknames included Gateway to Nowhere and Pigeons' Palace.

26 This is how many modern-day Dundonians would like to see their beloved but much maligned waterfront! Here is the Esplanade in 1907 (looking west) with all the elegance expected of Edwardian times. The popular promenade was opened as far as the railway bridge in 1875. The replacement bridge can be seen in the distance.

27. Another current concern in the city is the future of the Baxter Park pavilion, long the subject of neglect and the attention of vandals. Here, however, it is seen serving its original purpose, as the centrepiece of the formal park laid out in 1863 by Joseph Paxton, the man who also designed Chatsworth House and Crystal Palace. Baxter Park opened amid great rejoicing and a public holiday – but a planned balloon ascent in front of the assembled crowd of 60,000 failed to get off the ground because of wind speeds.

28 Magdalen Green has been a west end playground for two centuries. In times past the green ran down to the river to where an open-air bathing pool was sited. The tradition of dashing down to the shore came to an abrupt halt – literally – in 1845 with the arrival of the Perth to Dundee railway, an event which led to a protest by baptising ministers!

29 It is the boast – or threat – of the present Rector of Dundee High School that the last pupil of the school to be beheaded was the Scottish patriot Sir William Wallace! Punishments today are less drastic at a school which does much to add colour and energy to lunchtime Dundee. The principal school building, seen here, dates from 1834.

30 The historic Courier building, on the site of the old post office, was designed in 1902 and built of red Dumfries sandstone over four years. It is home to D.C. Thomson and Co, who publish a wide rang of newspapers and periodicals. Meadowside, in front of the building, was previously occupied by an assortment of retail sheds and booths.

31 This card, posted in August 1908, marks a brief visit to the city of Queen Alexandra and her daughter Princess Victoria. After spending the summer at Balmoral the Queen joined the Royal Yacht Victoria and Albert at Dundee. She was seen off by a full turn-out of civic dignitaries and thousands of members of the public – with the only paparazzi present being our pioneering postcard photographer.

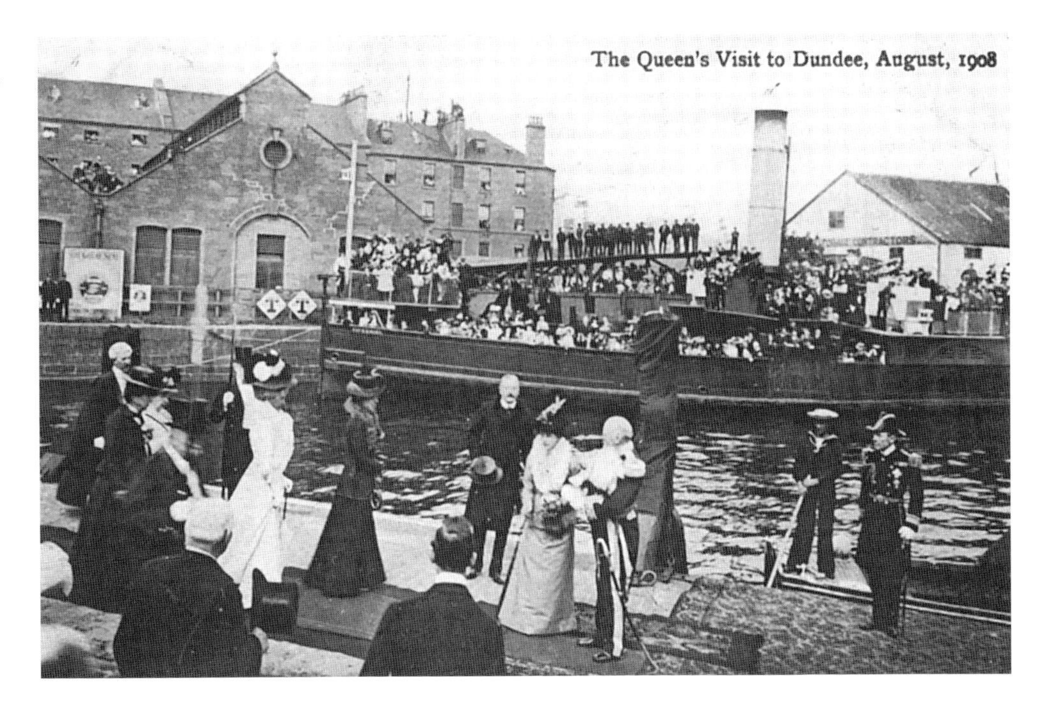

32. We now see the Queen's party from the opposite side of the harbour. Note the advertising hoardings far left, which have been carefully curtained off to protect delicate royal eyes!

Queen's Visit to Dundee.—Her Majesty stepping on board Pinnace

33 In Edwardian times, as now, Dundee Flower Show was a great event on the city's social calendar. The show was traditionally held on Magdalen Green, as shown on this card from 1905, and was normally opened by the Countess of Strathmore. Visitors would arrive by cab at the large tents erected on the park. Dundee Flower Show, as popular as ever, is now held at Camperdown Park.

34 King George V and Queen Mary visited Dundee in the summer of 1914. After arriving by train they toured the city in an open carriage, being greeted by large crowds along the way. This view shows the royal carriage passing down the richly-decorated Whitehall Street. 'This is a postcard for your album,' says the sender. How right he was!

35 We now see large crowds watching the royal progress down Commercial Street. In the background John Thomson's bar advertises Allsopp's Pale Ale and Watson's Whisky. Although Watson's bonded warehouse was in Dundee, whisky wasn't distilled in the city.

36 Here, schoolchildren in their Sunday best gather in Albert Square in readiness to march to the Esplanade to see off the royal visitors. By his stern look and soldier-like demeanour we can safely assume that the gentleman in the foreground is a teacher! All the children were given commemorative gifts to mark the occasion. Where are they now?

37 When the royal party arrived at the Keiller's factory in the centre of Dundee (now the Forum shopping centre) it was met by the sight and scent of specially created floral tributes and a banner proclaiming 'Keiller's Offer Loyal Greetings'.

38 Soldiers recuperate outside a First World War convalescent home at Magdalen Green, on this war-time postcard. When trains carrying wounded soldiers began arriving from the Front, such homes were quickly established and staffed by volunteers.

39 This early photograph, which captures the granting of the Freedom of the City to Lord Roberts in 1893, is memorable for its variety of hats! They range from the General's hat on the left, as worn by Lord Roberts, to the Lord Lieutenant's fine plumes next to him and the senior police officer's domed helmet opposite. In the background is an assortment of top hats, bowlers and bearskins – even a small lad in a sailor's cap.

40 'Dundee is not up to much,' said the sender of this card in 1909. Thankfully the postcard is; a stunning view across the Tay Bridge to Dundee. Wormit station in the foreground closed in 1969 – but there has been a determined campaign in recent years to re-establish a rail halt there.

41 A submarine base was constructed in Dundee in 1909 and, that year, twelve submarines, one gunboat, one parent ship, the Vulcan, and 600 naval personnel arrived in the city. The submariner tradition continued into the Second World War when Britain's biggest flotilla was based in Dundee, though its presence was shrouded in secrecy. By 1945 a multinational fleet of twenty vessels was tied up at King George Wharf.

42 The Mars Training Ship arrived on the Tay in 1869. Some 6,500 boys were ‘sent tae the Mars’ over the next sixty years. A book by Linda McGill in 1996 exploded some of the myths surrounding the ship, however. It was not a place for bad boys. And it was not home to Dundee boys. Often there were more boys aboard from Glasgow and Edinburgh. The ship itself was built as an 81-gun, four-deck man-of-war at Chatham in the 1840s.

43 Dundee's suffragettes played a remarkable role in the struggle to win votes for women. Militancy gathered pace in the years up to 1914. Windows in Dundee were smashed. Farington hall was burned down. There was an attempt to blow up Dudhope Castle. And, if collectors wonder why there might be a dearth of local postcards from 1913, it is possibly because radical suffragettes attacked postboxes throughout the city with fire, glue and corrosive chemicals!

44 'Dear Aunt. We have arrived in Dundee and this is our new address.' So says the sender of this fine 1911 Valentine's card showing Park Avenue. And, sure enough, the new address is duly marked with a thick black cross. Note the woman cleaning a window high on the left foreground.

45 The Courier Buildings are seen here flying flags and bunting to commemorate the Coronation of King George V in 1911. Just visible is the Lion Rampant flag on the building's main pole. The Lion Rampant has continued to be flown by the Dundee publishers to this day.

46 Seen on the right here is the former Ward Road Railway Station, prior to its demolition to make way for the new Post Office. The station was the city terminus of the Dundee & Newtyle Railway, which began in 1831. The line wound its way up from Ward Road up the side of the Law assisted by a stationary steam engine and ropes. From there it went through the Law tunnel and onward to the Sidlaws.

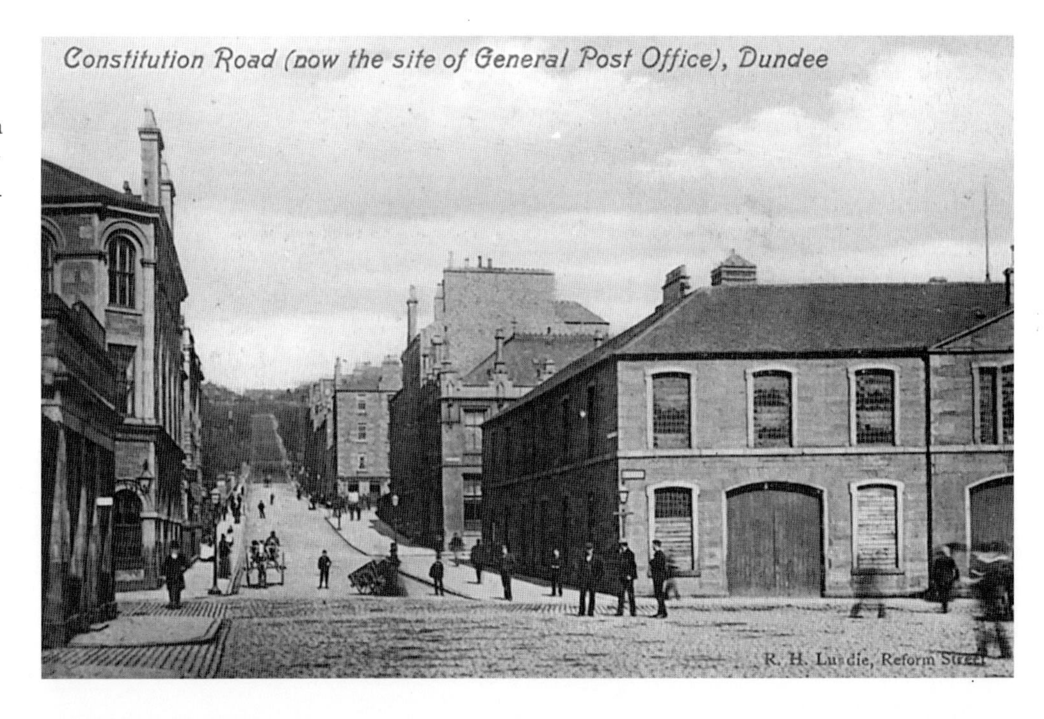

47 The foundation stone of the Caird Hall was laid by King George V on 10th July 1914. The ceremony was performed by 'electric connection' – the button pressed by the King being the famous Caird emerald, one of the world's biggest, which is now in the chain of office of the Lord Provost of Dundee. This commemorative card marks the opening of the hall and City Square in November 1933.

48 This fine view of the Murraygate, looking east towards the old Wellgate, harnesses the magical period when carts passed over transport's reins to trams which, in turn, gave way to motor vehicles. Prominent on the right is Duncan's shoe shop. The patrolling policeman, left, appears to be casting a suspicious glance at an abandoned crate.

49 One of Dundee's busiest suburbs is Stobswell. It was here in the early 20th century that fine new tenements were built to rehouse the city's slum dwellers. In the inter-war period alone, Dundee Corporation built 8,374 new houses. Morgan Academy already existed, of course. When, in 1863, it was decided to build the school, it was thought the maximum number of pupils would be 100!

50 A huge turn-out greeted a surprise visit by Sir James Ritchie, Lord Mayor of London, to Dundee in July 1904. It was, said the Dundee Advertiser, 'the first Lord Mayor's show in Dundee'. Two months later Sir James was created an honorary Dundee bonnetmaker.

51 This undated but unusual advertising card from the 1920s indicates that the 'combined circulation' of D.C. Thomson publications was in excess of three million copies weekly. Not bad for a firm which promoted 'penny dreadful' magazines for women mill workers and which, in 1866, produced the first halfpenny morning newspaper in Britain. Though perhaps there is an element of stage management in the array of transport passing head office!

52 Much is known of Captain Scott's Research Ship Discovery, now the star exhibit in the visitor centre bearing her name. But without the Terra Nova, the Discovery would never have returned from the Antarctic in 1904. The Terra Nova spent many years in Arctic waters before sailing south to assist Scott's ill-fated expedition. In 1909 she took Scott on his second and ultimately fatal expedition to the South Pole.
He never returned. His ship did, and sailed on until she was sunk in 1944.

S.S. "Terra Nova" (the "Discovery" Relief Ship)
Valentines Series

53 Although this cartoon card was sold in Walton-on-the-Naze, it depicts Dundee's only woman MP to date, Florence Horsbrugh.
In the early 1930s Horsbrugh led a vocal campaign to outlaw Red Biddy, a mixture of cheap wine and methylated spirits. She eventually succeeded in having an Act passed banning it from being sold, but not before publishers decided she was fair game for the postcard pun!

54 There were only so many ways to show Dundee's civic buildings on postcards. After every conceivable view was published, the next obvious step was to produce a set of Dundee in darkness, well, virtual darkness! This example appears to set out to demonstrate the power of the new electric light bulbs in the Albert Institute, among the first in the city.

55 A busy scene in the Murraygate. This is one of the oldest streets in Dundee. It is believed to have been named after Thomas Randolf, first Earl of Moray and nephew of King Robert the Bruce. It was Randolf, with only thirty men, who captured Edinburgh Castle from the English during the Wars of Independence in the 14th century.

56 We now move back a few yards into the High Street with the unmistakable Pillars on the right. Public executions were carried out in front of the Town House. When it was proposed to open a new street southwards from near this spot to the harbour in 1820, the house of Dr. Crichton, an eminent local surgeon, stood in the way. According to tradition, not until the civic fathers agreed to name the street after him did he agree to move!

57 The Scotia was one of Dundee's most famous whalers. Perhaps its greatest claim to nautical fame, however, is that it inaugurated the North Atlantic Ice Patrol in 1913, following the sinking of the Titanic. The Scotia wasn't a Dundee-built ship. She was launched in Norway in 1872 and probably spent her early life as a sealer in Greenland waters. She was eventually bought for the Scottish National Antarctic Expedition and sailed from Troon in 1902. She joined the Dundee whaling fleet two years later.

58 The planning of Reform Street coincided with the passing of the Reform Bill in 1832 and the street opened the following year. An alternative suggestion for its name was put forward by one town councillor. His idea was to call it Mortgage Street!

59 One of the most famous sights in Dundee was the mass evening exodus from the giant Camperdown Works in Lochee. The massive complex was begun by the Cox Brothers in 1849. In its heyday it was the largest jute mill in the world. In recent years the huge 33-acre site has been redeveloped to provide over 300 houses, as well as a major entertainment complex.

60 This fine view of the City Assembly Rooms in the late 1890s indicates how impressive a building it must have been in bygone days. Since then it has endured many changes of use but, thankfully, little in the way of alteration. Known for many years as the Winter's the Printers building, it has recently become a restaurant. Note the horse trough in the foreground.

61 The fire in Watson's Bond in the Seagate in July 1906 raged for two days and was believed to be one of Britain's biggest conflagrations. It led to the virtual destruction of one of Dundee's most prominent buildings. For several hours a flaming river of whisky flowed down the streets as a million gallons of spirits went up in smoke!

62 And what more would be required for a smart turn-out of Dundee's fire brigade than a major city centre fire? And here they are emerging from the new fire station in Bell Street. Curiously, this was virtually the entire Dundee fire service at the turn of the century – though some larger firms had their own part-time firemen.

63 St. Mary's Fair, or Lady Mary's Fair, was almost certainly Dundee's oldest. Although its history dates back several centuries it moved to the Greenmarket area of Shore Terrace (shown here) in 1907, where various amusements were sited, and where a weekly market already existed. When the building of the new Caird Hall encroached upon the Greenmarket site in 1914 the future of the fair was placed in jeopardy. It was eventually abolished in 1934.

64 This is a typical Dundee shop front postcard. It is, as was usual, awash with enamel signs – much sought after by collectors today – with staff posing for the photographer outside. Mrs. Burns' fruit and confectionery shop traded at 59 King Street and is seen in 1923.

65 Bucklemaker's Wynd was one of the principal streets in old Dundee – but it was so narrow that it was difficult for two jute carts to pass coming and going from mills to docks. So it was widened in the middle of the last century and became once again one of Dundee's most important thoroughfares – Victoria Road.

66 A fine study of Whitehall Crescent and Union Street. Note the 'taxi' conveying a woman passenger towards the High Street, perhaps to the new D. M. Brown arcade. The ladies of 1910 wore steel and bone, rampart-like corsets. But by and large it was a dainty era for girls.

67 This view of Whitehall Street, about 1900, shows full-skirted women on foot, and a glimpse of the famous Draffen's store on the right. Its full title then was Draffen & Jarvie, established by George Draffen and John Jarvie in 1889. It trades today as Debenham's.

68 In the days before direct charter flights to the sun, holiday-making Dundonians would more than likely find themselves here – on Broughty Ferry beach. Bank holiday excursions went further afield of course (sometimes as far as Perth!) but there was nothing to top a trip to 'the Ferry'.

At the Beach, Broughty Ferry

69 Dundee docks, under the careful watch of the Dock-master's office (left fore-ground). To the left was Earl Grey Dock which stretched along the shore to where Captain Scott's research ship Discovery is now berthed. When Discovery was launched in 1901 a special luncheon was held in the Queen's Hotel, hosted by the ship's makers, Dundee Shipbuilders Co. Ltd.

70 Gray Street, Broughty Ferry, without a car in sight! No double yellow lines, no lights, no cable television workmen digging up the streets. It is a pity that we have to turn back the clock some ninety years to witness such a scene!

71 The Union Hall in the old Nethergate was a church originally. It was constructed in 1783 and existed for almost a century before being demolished as part of the city's radical improvement scheme during the 1870s. Note the size of the clock.

72 Prior to the construction of George V Wharf, King William Dock (shown here), along with Earl Grey Dock, was often lined with vessels loading or discharging. On the street side, cargoes of timber from the Baltic would be discharged directly on to railway wagons from the tall sailing ships and barges. This dock became home to Dundee's whaling fleet.

73 It is possible that this is a demonstration parade during the acrimonious dockers' and carters' strike of 1911. This strike paralysed trade in Dundee and led to the closure of more than twenty mills with 20,000 people laid off from work. Three hundred Black Watch soldiers were deployed to keep the peace, along with hundreds of policemen. Despite this, there were various disturbances as the men pressed claims for better working conditions and improved pay.

74 Dundee's history is entwined with efforts to span the Tay estuary. The first Tay Bridge was designed by Thomas Bouch (1822-1880). This postcard shows the girders of the first bridge (top), along with some of the girders used in the construction of its eventual replacement.

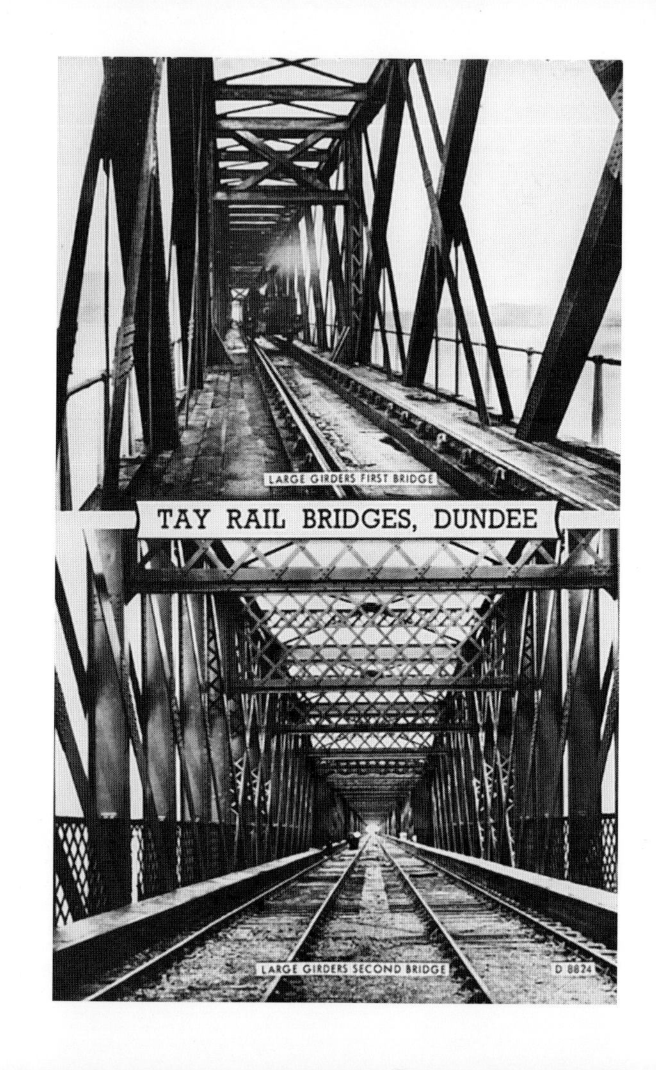

75 Bouch's rail crossing over the Tay was opened in May, 1878. Just 18 months later, after a terrible storm on 28th December 1879, the city woke up to the sight of a yawning gap at the centre of the bridge and the news that up to 75 people had been lost, presumed drowned, after a passenger train plunged into the water. This card, published when the disaster must have been fresh in the minds of many, shows the protruding piers of the bridge.

76 For Fifers, too, the collapse of the Tay Bridge in the storm of 1879 must have taken on nightmarish proportions. This postcard shows the view seen by the people of Wormit as the morning of 29th December dawned.

77 We now see a comparison of the old and new Tay bridges, with the dual pillars of the new bridge clearly defined. Inquiries into the collapse of the first bridge found that the soil composition of the river bed was incapable of taking the load weight of solid iron girders on a solid masonry base. Also, it was asserted that wind resistance factors were incorrectly calculated.

78 This close-up view of the construction of the new bridge in 1886 shows its proximity to the stone piers of the first bridge. The second bridge was constructed by William Arrol of Glasgow and opened for service in 1887. Fourteen men lost their lives during its construction.

79 And so we see the Tay Bridge as it stands today – though steam trains passing over it are something of a rarity, sad to say. In the foreground is the area of former playground now occupied by a garage showroom and bowling green – but internationally known as the view from James McIntosh Patrick's studio!

80 D. M. Brown's arcade was opened on 3rd December 1908. 'Taken as a whole,' said the Dundee Advertiser, 'the arcade excels anything of the kind in Scotland, if indeed it is equalled by anything in Britain.' One of the attractions of the new arcade was its sophistication. The newspaper alluded to this aspect: 'Through the pneumatic tubes with which every section of the establishment is connected to a central exchange in the basement, the cash clatters with exactness and despatch.'

81 The old Custom House was one of a number of mansions that graced Fish Street and Butcher Row, an aristocratic quarter of 17th century Dundee. The Custom House was closed in 1803. When it was partly demolished five years later, some 200 coins dating to the reigns of James VI and Charles I were discovered. They were believed to have been concealed in the building by an inhabitant who perished in the siege of the city by General Monk in 1651.

82 The fire at Watson's Bond in the Seagate in July 1906 was described by The Courier as 'the most destructive fire in the history of Dundee'. The fire raged for twelve hours, burned for two days, destroyed the huge bonded warehouse and consumed millions of gallons of spirit. The paper reported 'panic' in Candle Lane as the flames spread and 'rivers of burning whisky' flowed down the streets.

83 This Tuck's Oilette art card by local illustrator David Small, about 1906, helps to indicate the stark intrusion on the harbour skyline of the controversial Royal Arch. The death sentence had hung over the arch for many years, but the execution order didn't come until February 1964 when Duncan Logan, the Tay Road Bridge builders, announced the start of demolition. Given its unhappy existence and ultimate fate, it is remarkable that there were 148 entries in the design competition to build it.

84 Another postcard from the Tuck's Oilette series shows Dundee's Greenmarket in full swing around 1906. The First World War drew many of the traders and market-goers into the Armed Services and levels of trading dropped. But what had a greater impact on the future of the market was the encroachment of the new Caird Hall, whose construction had begun in 1913. The final nail in the Greenmarket's coffin came in 1935 when it made way for Shore Terrace bus station.

85 The solemn Caird Hall façade is seen in this Valentine's postcard published shortly after the hall opened in 1923. Yet there was provision under the rear of the £100,000 hall for a jumble of permanent stalls, and this duly became the City Arcade. Many Dundonians, mourning the loss of the Greenmarket, felt this compromise was simply the result of a covert civic plan to abolish the city's open-air markets.

86 From the roof of the Caird Hall, a more modern postcard provides a panoramic view of the summer-time city. Note the flower arrangements in the foreground, which bear a passing resemblance to the 'environmental improvements' of recent years. Another point of interest is the traffic on both sides of the square, while, in the background, the two corner sites are occupied by the retailers present today, Boots and H. Samuel.

87 This rare postcard shows the tug Bullger manoeuvring into position to tow the Mars Training Ship down the Tay and to the scrapyards at Inverkeithing. The Mars had given sixty stout years of service. And she was made of stern stuff. Oxy-acetylene burners and steel cutters made little impact on her two-feet thick oak timbers. Explosives eventually provided the former warship with a dignified end.

88 This fine study shows the Eastern Medical Hall next to the Victoria Bar at the top of Victoria Road. The greatest character in this vicinity was Edwin Scrymgeour, Britain's only Prohibitionist MP, who lived in a close in Errol Terrace, just off Victoria Road. After his victory over Winston Churchill in 1922 ‘Neddy’ remarked to hundreds of supporters who had followed him home up the brae: ‘Can ony o’ you fowk imagine your MP bidin’ up a closie?’

89 We now look over Albert Square towards the High School of Dundee. Early in the 13th century Earl Gilbert, Bishop of Brechin, granted the abbot and monks of Lindores permission to establish a school in Dundee. Famous early pupils of the school were the Scottish patriot Sir William Wallace and the 16th-century historian Hector Boece, who became the first principal of Aberdeen University.

90 Dundee's David Small (1846-1927) is again the artist for this romanticised Oilette of Mains Castle. The castle was completed in 1582 and came into the possession of jute baron Sir James Caird in 1912. Although Sir James died soon after, the restoration of the castle was completed by his sister Mrs. Marryat, and it was she who opened Caird Park to the public that year.

91 This fine Valentine's study of Castle Court probably dates from the 1870s, though in postcard form it was retailed by R. H. Lundie of Reform Street well into the 20th century. Nestling under the spire of St. Paul's Cathedral, this view of Castle Court provides an insight into typical housing conditions endured by Dundee's Victorian working class – and the type of housing heavily criticised by Dundee Social Union's ground-breaking report into the city's health and sanitary conditions in 1905.

92 How imposing Dundee Royal Infirmary must have looked when it was newly constructed in the 1850s. Hemmed in by buildings on three sides today and now close to closure, the DRI in Barrack Road was originally a replacement for the former city hospital in King Street.

93 One wonders what environmental health officers today would make of this scene! But in Edwardian Dundee the city's shopkeepers proudly displayed their wares – and were happy to pose for the pioneering postcard photographer. On display here, along with the high class ham, is Wm Grant & Son of the West Port.

94 The Frigate Unicorn, today berthed in Victoria Dock, is one of the oldest ships afloat in the world and a sparkling jewel in Dundee's tourism crown. Here the ship is lit up in honour of the Coronation of 1953. This postcard, issued by the Unicorn Preservation Society, was published when the ship was known as HMS Cressy.

95 In another card from the series we see the upper deck inside the ship. Looking aft we see the capstan and the ship's wheel. The Unicorn's distinctive wooden roof was added in 1873 when she was brought to Dundee. The Unicorn was launched at Chatham in 1824.

96 The roof of the Old Town House provides the perfect position to view the heart of old Dundee. The Nethergate goes off to the left, below the spire of St. Paul's Church. In the middle distance, in shadow,

Thorter Row goes off to the right. And on the right the much-loved old Overgate is glimpsed. With the to- and fro-ing of the trams and huge advertising hoardings isn't there just a hint of Piccadilly Circus?

97 The Vault was an ancient lane which was situated west of the Town House. It took its name from an old gateway to St. Clement's kirkyard which formerly opened to the harbour. There were several old houses in former times which were considered of great civic importance. One of them, an oak-panelled mansion with a fine staircase, was the town house of the Lords of Strathmartine.

98 By the late 1820s Dundee had only two terraced developments of note, one in King Street and one in Tay Street. Then Windsor Street, seen here, was laid out in the finest Georgian traditions, providing a fine panorama over the estuary to Fife. Windsor Street marked the western edge of the town when it was built. Today, it is virtually part of the city centre!

99 This imposing steam-driven tram dates from around 1895 and served on the Baxter Park to Lochee route. We see it at the Commercial Street, High Street, Murraygate junction. Note the advertisement for the Evening Telegraph, only $^1/_2$d! In the background is G.W. Wilson, known to all in Dundee as 'The Corner'. Steam traction was first used in Dundee on the Lochee tram route in 1885.

100 More trams! Here we see an electric tram in the High Street en route to Downfield. But the foreground is taken up by horse and carts, the mainstay of trade transport in Dundee in the early 1900s. This postcard provides an interesting profile of the Pillars, or Town House, which was controversially demolished in 1932. Beneath the arches at this time were shops such as Braithwaite's the coffee merchant, McLean the tobacconist, Bruce the confectioner and Littlejohn the newsagent.

101 And to prove this transport point, this view of the High Street, taken much earlier, shows a complete absence of mechanised vehicle! The presence of the old Trades Hall in the background, now the site of the elegant Clydesdale Bank building, helps us to date this Valentine's photograph to some time before 1878.

102 Moving on thirty years, we can see the transformation of the Murraygate. The Trades Hall has been superceded by the new bank on the right. On the left, D. M. Brown's new arcade, with Wilson's Corner on the opposite side of Commercial Street, provide a hub for shoppers from miles around. D. M. Brown was taken over by House of Fraser in 1952.

103 This postcard marks the visit to Dundee of the Prince of Wales in October 1923, when he formally opened the new Caird Hall. Here he is seen in the leading motor car with Lord Provost Spence. The Dundee Advertiser, describing the visit, said, 'a touch of comedy which greatly tickled the Prince was provided at the entrance to the Seaforths' Club (in Park Place) by an old woman. Grasping the prince by the arm, she said: "Eh, laddie, are ye no' thinking of takin' a wife?"' Ironically, it was the matter of matrimony which led the Prince to abdicate in later years.

104 The Prince of Wales is seen leaving the Caird Hall in procession along Whitehall Crescent after an opening ceremony performed in front of an invited audience of 3,500. Among others, he was introduced to James Thomson, the city architect, and designer of the new hall. The Prince had previously visited the Royal Dundee Institution for the Blind and the Ashton Works in the Hawkhill.

105 This turn-of-the-century card shows the famous Eternity Stone in Annan Terrace, Wellington Street. The street was named after Robert Annan (1834-1867), who devoted his mature years to helping others. Twelve times he is said to have plunged into the waters of the Tay to save individuals from drowning. He died by drowning himself while attempting to save an 11-year-old boy. On the very day he died, Annan inexplicably wrote on a board at the door of his house, 'Where will you spend Eternity?' and then scribbled on the pavement the word 'Eternity' and the word 'Death' on his gate.

106 As whales became scarcer in the Arctic, the managers of the Dundee whaling fleet decided to explore the Antarctic. A four-ship expedition sailed south during the Antarctic summer of 1892-1893. The Balaena's shown here, along with the Active, Diana and Star, found the southern polar whales too large for the small Dundee ships. The Balaena was the first merchant ship to reach Franz Joseph Land. She was later stuck in ice for eighty days in Melville Bay in the Arctic.

107 The windjammer Lochee was the first ship of the Clipper Line and was launched from Stephen's yard at Marine Parade. At 1,812 tons, she was the largest sailing ship built on the Tay to that time. In 1882 she reached Dundee in ninety days from Calcutta, still the record under sail.

108 Here we can join in a gym class at Dundee High School, about 1896. The gymnasium was constructed in a new block at the rear of the main building and came about through the generosity of ex-Provost William Robertson, one of the school's staunchest supporters in its struggle for independence with Dundee School Board. Note the pose of the master on the right.

109 Now stroll across to Euclid Crescent in 1896 and join in the senior girls' art class. The girls' school was built in two stages between 1886 and 1890. The building site cost £10,000, a considerable amount compared to total building costs of £15,000. The girls appear to be modelling in clay.

110 This photograph dates from 1900 and shows a different class in a different school; this time the infant class at Harris Academy, Park Place. The nature of the subject being taught is something of a mystery. As the teacher plays the piano, the children pretend to be asleep. But the girl who is standing in front of a wooden abacus, appears to be pointing to a map.

111 Had logic not prevailed, the Nethergate, one of Dundee's most prominent shopping streets, might have been named the Flukergait. The Nethergate was once an area associated with fish and fishing and many knew it as the Flukergait, the word fluke being another word for flounder. This card, by the London publishers Davidson Brothers, shows the Nethergate looking west.

112 We now look down the Nethergate with the Moon, Langlands & Co. department store at the top of Union Street on the right. Even in Edwardian times, Union Street was a far cry from the days when a row of white-washed, thatched cottages formed a narrow thoroughfare leading from the harbour to the city churches. As rapid industrialisation occurred and railway termini were constructed nearby, Union Street is said to have seen many a Saturday night fight between soldiers passing in and out of the city. Often Bell Street jail was so full that offenders were told to come back the next morning!

113 Green's magnificent playhouse in the Nethergate opened on 4th March 1936 amid great publicity over its 'no expense spared' decor. Glass and marble were used lavishly, seating was upholstered in velvet, spotlights illuminated the gold walls, screen curtains were fashioned out of silk and satin. Above all this was its famous art deco steel, concrete and glass tower, which, when fully illuminated, was visible for miles.

114 One of the great attractions of Green's was the Sunshine Café, which could seat hundreds of patrons – perhaps as they waited with anticipation for the afternoon matinee. Alas, as cinema audiences fell dramatically in the 1960s, the Playhouse became a bingo hall. The building was destroyed by fire in 1995.

115 This Valentine's 'real photo' card from 1903 shows one of Dundee's most famous junctions – the Sinderins – where, looking east, Perth road bears to the right, and the Hawkhill goes off to the left. The approaching tram was on the High Street-Ninewells route. Of course, the Sinderins was known to all as The Sunderance.

116 One of the interesting facets of the 'developing' photographic industry was the pioneering approach of postcard publishers. Composite cards were issued on the Continent soon after view cards were allowed by the postal authorities in 1895. It didn't take major British publishers, such as Valentine's of Dundee, long to produce multi-view cards of every major town in the Kingdom. It was also economically expedient, as the views had invariably been issued previously as single cards!

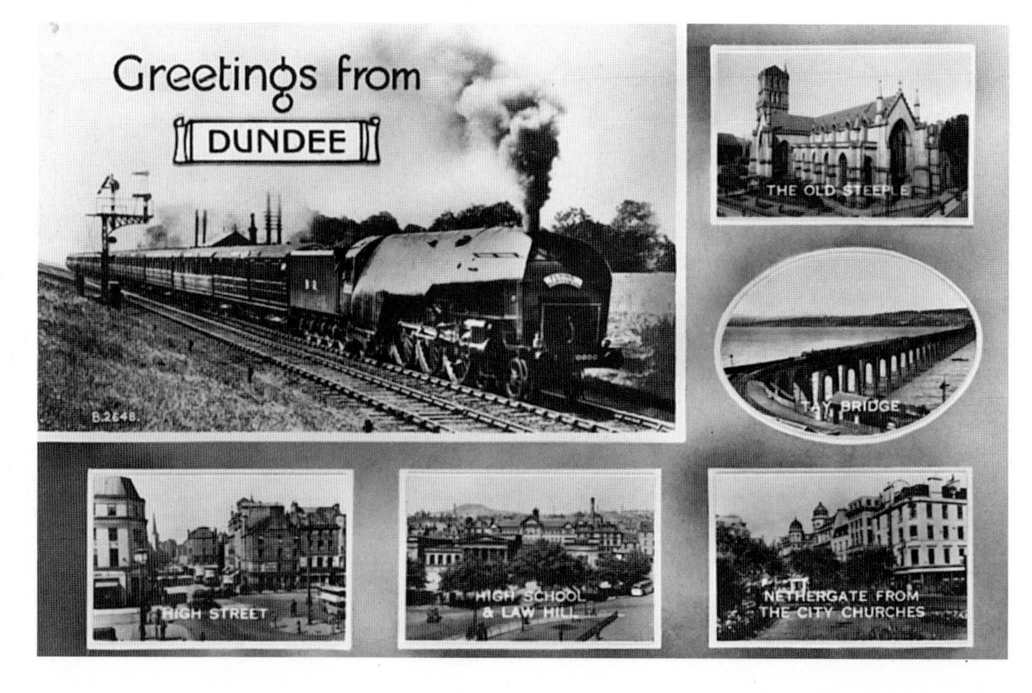

117 The location where Dundee witch Grizzel Jaffray was burned at the stake was commemorated by a circle of cobble stones in the Seagate. Jaffray was convicted of being in league with the Devil in November, 1669. Just before she died, she claimed there were other witches in Dundee, but no further executions took place. It is said her son, a mariner, sailed into Dundee on the day of her death. On learning of the commotion in the Seagate, he set sail from the harbour, never to return to Dundee.

118 Dundee's citizens queue to pledge their names to buy British war bonds. After five years of war, the Ministry of Defence arranged for a tank to tour the country as a means of encouraging people to buy citizen's bonds. Dundee Tank Week took place in February, 1918. The amount raised in Dundee in one week was a remarkable £4.5 million, a figure surpassed by only three cities in Britain.

119 We are well-used nowadays to American 'imports' such as surfing, skateboarding and in-line rollerskating. Things were much the same at the turn of the century as this wonderful postcard indicates. 'The latest craze' in Dundee, it reveals, is American rollerskating!

120 Dundee's trams in winter could be dark, shaky and cold, but generally they kept to their rails and their timetables when snow fell, unlike today's buses on occasion! Here we see trams, line astern, making their way along Main Street. Ironically, the wall advertisement on the far right is for 'winter woollies'! Dundee's trams reached their maximum passenger total in 1948, when they carried over 37 million people.

121 Now we see the Nethergate in the height of a blizzard with the east-bound High Street tram (left) about to pass the West Park tram (right). Some of the worst snow ever seen in Dundee occurred fifty years ago in 1947. At its worst, some 900 men were employed to clear Dundee's 180 miles of streets. At one point seven dozen spades and shovels were being returned to the cleansing department on a daily basis for repair.

122 This example from the rare advertising cards issued by D. C. Thomson differs from the Thomson Publications card already shown in that it features the company's London office, which it still retains at 185 Fleet Street, the Glasgow office where the Sunday Post is printed, and the company's Manchester office which closed recently. This card boasts over three million copies sold weekly. By 1964 this had exceeded 12 million copies weekly.

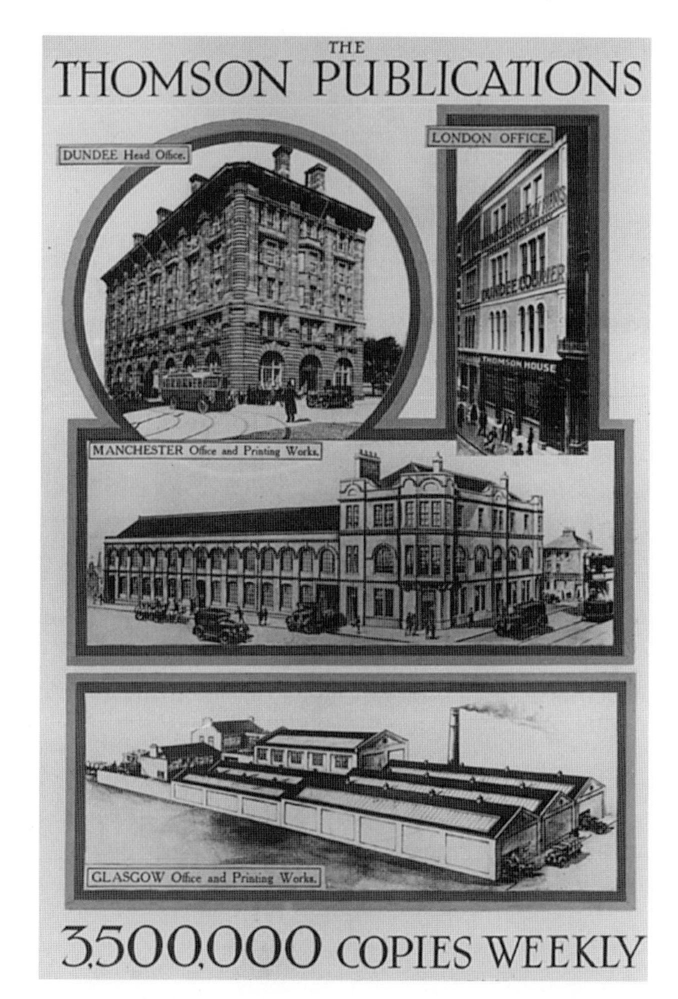

123 Note the extent of the cobble stones on this photograph of Dundee Auction Rooms in Ward Road about 1900. Adjacent was the famous Ward Road gymnasium. This building, opened in 1891, featured a sculptured relief above its front door representing the reclining figure of 'Mother Dundee' surrounded by a group of healthy, hearty children, representing the beneficial powers of gymnastics!

124 The origins of the Old Steeple and City Churches in Dundee are surrounded in mystery. Legend says that David, Earl of Huntingdon and brother of King William the Lion of Scotland, prayed to St. Mary for mercy as a violent storm threatened to swamp his ship and turn his return from the Crusades to tragedy. His prayers were answered. The Earl was washed up on the shores of the tiny community of Dundee around the year 1190. He kept his word, consecrating a church to St. Mary on the site of the present Steeple.

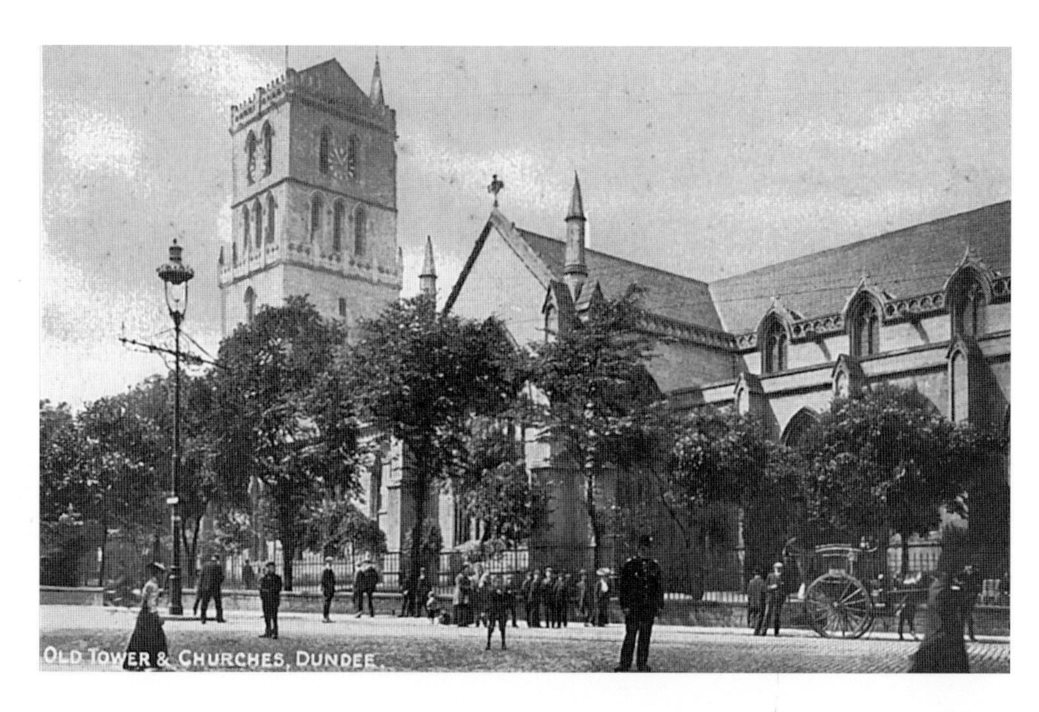

125 This fine study of Strathmartine Road, about 1905, reflects the changing character of Dundee at the turn of the century. The 1900 Dundee Year Book refers to the fact that, 'It is a pleasing commentary on the extension of the city's tramway service that many of the new buildings have been erected along those routes tapped by the new lines or in the vicinity of their termini'. In truth, the availability of transport infrastructure often dictated the new locations of Dundee's working population – and not the reverse.

126 The biggest impact on transport in Dundee in the 20th century was the creation and opening of the Tay Road Bridge. The possibility of such a bridge had been discussed as early as the 1920s, but it was only in 1955 that a Tay Road Bridge Joint Committee was established to investigate sites, costs and sources of finance.

127 Building the bridge began in March 1963 and the bridge was opened to traffic in August 1966. Its total cost was £6 million. The Tay Ferries service, of course, was an immediate casualty, and when the bridge was opened the service was withdrawn.

128 This busy scene of Gray Street, Broughty Ferry, about 1900, is a reminder of its one-time independent burgh status. Annexation proceedings were started in 1913. Dundee argued that the two communities were in reality one, and that if their application to administer Broughty Ferry was rejected Dundee couldn't expand. After a long and costly fight, which passed to the House of Commons, the decision went in Dundee's favour. Curiously, the Dundee jute barons, who lived in Broughty Ferry mansions, opposed the annexation.

129 Life on Broughty Ferry esplanade has also changed down the years. Today's younger generation meet for ice cream and the latest gossip. This Valentine's photograph, from the 1890s, shows a young boy mending nets and two women shelling mussels. Note the Ferry's own inshore fishing fleet in the background.

130 Another card by Valentine's shows a montage of scenes from the Tay Bridge tragedy of 1879. Disaster postcards were common in Edwardian times. Local fires, floods, mining disasters, train, tram or aeroplane crashes, earthquakes and shipping tragedies – all were captured by postcard photographers.

131 Dundee enjoys a sophisticated swimming and leisure centre with flumes and fitness facilities. Yesteryear, the city's Central Baths, virtually on the site of the new complex, looked somewhat more austere. This is the building seen from the west – but the interior was quite sumptuous, for those who could pay!

CENTRAL BATHS, WEST PROTECTION WALL
(From the West)

132 This is described as the First Class Private Bathroom. The facilities included second and third class changing; in the bad old days the third class being little more than a row of cold showers! Here, however, there is a fine porcelain bathroom suite, complete with what looks like a large back scrubber in the bath!

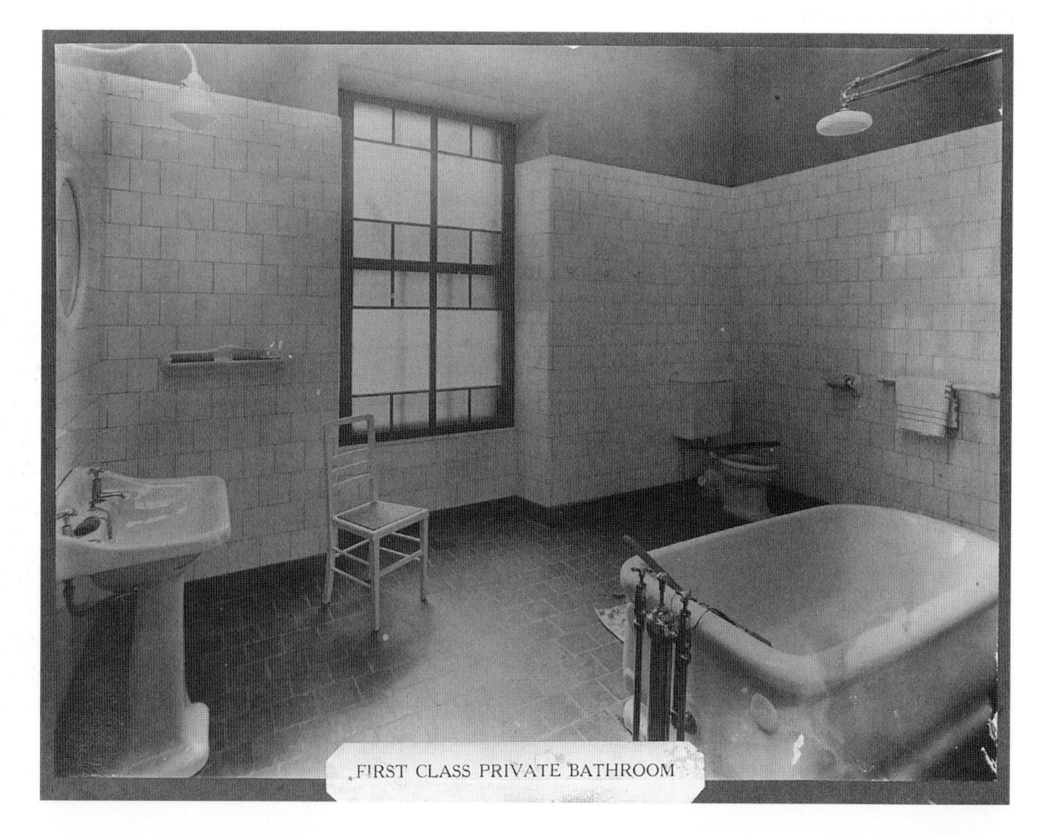
FIRST CLASS PRIVATE BATHROOM

133 Here we see the junction of Bell Street and Constitution Road. Prominent on the right is the YMCA building. Beyond is the tower of the Central Reading Room, now Barrack Street Museum. The basement flat seen on the right foreground in Constitution Road was the scene of a terrible tragedy in 1865 when twenty people were crushed to death, or suffocated, when a mass of people attending a concert fell down the steps and were trampled.

134 Slightly less macabre, this building at the corner of Larch Street and Cherryfield Lane was said to be haunted. By 1891 the output of tenement buildings like these was enormous – the census that year noted 233 blocks being built. This state of affairs came to an abrupt end in 1900 for the best of reasons – a shortage of tenants!

135 The original Royal Arch is seen here in this sketch from September 1844, which shows Queen Victoria's arrival at Dundee harbour. The temporary nature of the arch, which was hurriedly constructed in wood, was due to the sudden announcement of the royal visit. A more permanent sandstone arch replaced it in 1850.

136 Looking east along Dock Street we see the second Royal Arch in profile. On the left is Shore Terrace bus station which was removed in the early 1970s to make way for the Tayside Regional Council's tower-block headquarters. Some say the bus station was more attractive! Three prominent buildings seen here remain to this day – Caird Hall glimpsed on the left, the former Winter's print house in the centre, and Custom House in the right background.

137 Standing on the corner of High Street and Castle Street was the Royal British Hotel, now the University of Dundee Chalmers Hall. More interesting, perhaps, is the once common sight of a Keiller's shop. The name Keiller is synonymous with Dundee. Factory production of their famous Dundee marmalade began in 1797. As its popularity 'spread' it moved to larger premises in Albert Square, then to a huge factory in Maryfield. In 1971 the former Albert Square site became a shopping complex bearing the Keiller name.

138 A prominent building today in the transformed East Port area of Dundee is the former Blackscroft Library. It is seen here on the right of a photograph taken in the 1930s, which serves to indicate how tenements once confined Dundee's considerable population to the city centre, prior to the building of large peripheral estates. In the densest areas some 6,000 people per 100 acres were accommodated. In places like Barnhill and Broughty Ferry, however, the figure was around 400 per 100 acres.

139 This wonderful photograph shows a war-time procession of decorated floats along Broughty Ferry esplanade. Since the annexation of the burgh by Dundee in 1913 the people of Broughty Ferry had expected 'compensation' in the form of an outdoor swimming pool on the sea front. After over twenty years of discussions, however, a joint sub-committee of Dundee council voted in January 1937 to abandon the scheme.

140 And finally – we end with a typical Edwardian 'heraldic' postcard showing Dundee's coat of arms. The historic insignia has undergone several changes over the centuries, but the famous pot of lilies, a symbol of purity, which represent the ancient links to St. Mary, remain at its heart.